SHADES OF MAYBE

A Collection of Poetry and
Illustrations by

Luke Rawnsley

CONTENTS

The Yangtze River
The Green
Barbed Wire
Shades of maybe
Enough
The Let Go
Skint & Beerless
The Child
Flake
Filthy Fivers
Roach
Umbra
The Fist
The Keel
The Abyss
Dancing and Sitting
The Sun on my Back
Black and Black
Farewell Mother Farewell

THE YANGTZE RIVER

The Yangtze River
Deep and wide
Starting as a trickle
She bent her way
Through soft earth
She gained her strength
Pushing through stones
Her very ambition
Carved through mountains
Driven by the unseen
She became magnificent
Bringing life with her
The millennia passed by
A fleeting reflection
Off her ever moving back
She writhed snakelike
Shaking off any purchase
She grew lazy and fat
Forgot the small steps
As she wound ever forward

Men came and marvelled
She was legend and song
So mysterious and vast
To swallow every man
And not show a ripple
From her huge consumption
From old to young
Reputation instant and known
She lay in satisfaction
That no man or beast
Could ever know her
Or ever chart her course
A blink of her slow eye
And empires rose and fell
She remained still unknown
Until a tickle of her tail
She tries to look back
Magnitude stops her gaze
But she can feel something
That she forgot an eon ago
Ambition stirs far away
To match her very own

It's path is alongside her
Step following every drop
It's eyes are on her
With more than mild curiosity
Day by day it follows
She can't shake the feeling
That she will become known
Surely mountain and moor
Will break its gaze
Or savage claw or beak
Wrestle and break its intent
And yet it walks at side
It never tires or slows to stop
For the first time ever
Yangtze can see the day
Time slows to each moment
She captures alien reflection
Of this strange creature
That won't let her be
Whose spirit is as strong
As the cuddling land
That presses to her side

It's follows still onward
As if seen its resting head
A sureness of path as her own
They both now move as one
Each expectant of the other
Was she made for this?
An impossible test for creation
Where fear sinks through surface
Like the stones dropped in her
Is she the maker of legends?
The tamer becoming tamed
Even fold and crease of time
Will be stretched like canvass
For everyone to paint a mark
And yet she feels the respect
Feels its love grow stronger
As she bends her body away
As if to dislodge its grip
And stronger still it seems
It longs to lay eyes on her
When it's not by her side
Over the blinking of her eye

They are somehow now friends
Even though she has now changed
He remembers her childhood
Recalls the days she was lost
A tiny trickle twisting in shadow
She will share her legend briefly
Be known and loved in entirety
They will share the same story
Be gathered together in song
Sang as one and the same
Be whispers and rumours
Until as deafening as her might
Memory of their journey
Will always be known.

The Yangtze River is dedicated to Ash Dykes, the Guinness World Record holder as the first person to walk the entire length of the Yangtze River from source to sea.

THE GREEN

I surrendered to it before
The green grass I mean
I watched it gather pace
Until my eyes were green

It was bigger than me
When the wind hit it
It moved like a sea
Growing into all before it

It even waited in dreams
Pressing itself through the grey
The grey endless sleeps
Door jams to all the dull

Thick blades conceal me
I am wandering aimlessly
Blind to even my hands
That push through the grass

I feel my old lives briefly

Read books and furniture edges
Touch my hands then gone
Brushing against skin and mind

The grass grows thicker still
Pressing through my eyelids
Sinks like ink into my veins
Greens up my very arteries

I draw breath for the forests
Whose leaves now garment me
Shouldered burdens of bark
Coat my movements and hold

Stopping now in the glade
All direction is but a fantasy
As I take root among this riot
Of colours and seasoned rhyme

I am now gnarled twisted stem
Whose tears mix with the rain
Up to neck in soft warm earth
Peeking through the undergrowth

I see the old lives and silhouettes
Lost chance and fleeting fortune
Bend away to unfamiliar horizons
Heels covered by the rabid grass

I'm underfoot and all but forgot
To the passing of heal and toe
That will one day join me here
Amongst this lush green platform

I enjoyed this grass too once
The bounce of fevered motion
Pirouette of eternal abandon
Twisting between daisy and dew.

SHADES OF MAYBE

BARBED WIRE

A broken fence leans out
Barbed wire mesh slithered on it
Sitting in a bed of baked old asphalt
Shadowed by a heavily rusted car
The man gathers his thoughts
He squints toward the horizon
Inside the heat shimmer it flickers
A chrome reflection of a Chevrolet
Coming steadily toward him
His battered suitcase feels heavier
Holding his past by a leather strap
He takes a deep breath of dry air
The car slows to a squeaking halt
She is waiting her face shows it
Her soft lips press on hard words
He walks to the passenger side
Tentatively pulling the door open
They move off gathering speed
The dusty road spits up stones
The desert passes the window

Like a roll of dirty sandpaper
It scours away every last softness
The words between them are few
Brittle offerings that hold no hope
The years between them are gone
They both hold each other's breath
Neither one prepared to exhale
The moments tiptoe past them
He slowly looks sideways at her
He notices she is still beautiful
Despite all the darkness she glows
There should be no sunrise and yet
Her voice has become softer now
It's dulcet tones warming his mind
She is talking of forgiveness again
He listens for the first time ever
Despite it all she is breaking him
Not with hammers but with soft words
Knots of tension untwist in him
He tastes salt at his mouths corner
His own tears a gathered reminder
He loved you just remember that

Yet it was a memory that had faded
Time had rubbed away at the detail
They are walking away from the car
Past a newly painted iron railing
His mother's pace slows slightly
The years have caught up and cling
A breeze buffets them from behind
Wafting hints of cherry blossom
They follow the worn-down pathway
Past the stories written in stone
Standing apart each side of it
They look down and read the script
For my son you are the reason why
I had hope and capacity to love
May our good memories be enough
That you will always find the light.
All my love,
Dad.

SHADES OF MAYBE

SHADES OF MAYBE

The sky paints shades of maybe
Gathered restless clouds aplenty
Reflected on the bustling stream
The trickling knee carries the beam
Of sunlight that slaps white heat
Of wind hassled fern and cut peat
The watchful hare coiled unsprung
Of winged assault to burning lung
Pierce and shrill hawks battle song
To lift limb as to rattle dinner gong
Restless eye picks up faint heart
The game afoot now both play part
Gambling hare shows its hand
Guiding both skills of air and land
Death drops from the vaulted seam
Time punctured like waking dream
Terrible speed blurs focus of will
Of chaotic endeavour evading kill
Yet talon and beak neither to feast
As prey contorts to find the crease

Feathered fury is denied its claim
As sanctuary still twists its frame
Turn of foot and the chance is lost
A footprints testament in the frost

ENOUGH

There is no end to see
There is no darkening
There is no shade
There is no shadow
There is no light
There is no colour
There is no warm
There is no chill
There is no turmoil
There is no calm
There is no anger
There is no fear
There is no quickening
There is no pause
There is no hesitation
There is no wait
There is no sigh
There is no tear
There is no regret
There is no pain

There is you

There is me

There are moments

There are dreams

There are smiles

There are friends

There are lovers

These things are

These things are not

These things are abundant

These things are few

These things don't define

These things don't mark

These things are held

These things are lost

There are no words

There are no shapes

There are no sounds

There is only you

Holding my hand

And that is enough

LUKE RAWNSLEY

THE LET GO

Break the stem of reason
It should not have ambition for sky
Or any need of earth
Forget all the comfort that exists
Stroking the underbelly of fear
Touch your scars tenderly
But for no longer than their length
Drown in helplessness a little
While swimming toward the shore
Lay the pieces of heart and mind
Across the path of friend and foe
Let go of all that matters this day

LUKE RAWNSLEY

SKINT & BEERLESS

Skint and beerless

We would squander our time at a
place called the basin

We was young enough to be fearless

And didn't care what we was facin'

And as for Jason he be misplacin'

A simple distrust of authority

That came from the power of a minority

Crushing the dreams of a majority

And left us to rot on council estates

Where we had nothin' on our plates

Except the expectation of that in a few years

We could rap about the life we was hatin'

It was a given in fact doubtless that

The world still spun with or without us

But anyway I ain't no bleeding heart

I simply wanna tear apart

The misconception that just cos
your life starts out bad

And your sad or mad
Like your cousin, mum or dad
They're not a reflection of what's inside you
They are just the lessons of the classes you walk thru

Let's be real and get back to basics
We'd all rather be wearing Reebok
Then a pair of Asics
A little trip down memory lane
Past the bus stop I set aflame
Me and my mate would hit the arcade
Bunking off from school
Hiding the blazers that gave us away
Dropping pieces on space invaders
From the pack of family size quavers
That his aunt previously gave us
Once we nicked a trolley from the local supermarket
It wasn't our usual mode of transport
And we didn't know where to park it
So we took it up Finsbury hill
And let off the brakes
Watching thru cheers and tears

'So this is the damage it makes'

Then we scraped together our change
And set off for the chippy
Hoping we had enough
to get full from our one pound fifty
After we would watch kung fu vids
Pretending we were martial artists
Instead of little kids
Or he'd be Luke Skywalker
And me of course Darth Vader
And if he beat me with a light sabre
I would tease him about his sister
and the hickey I gave her
And if it ended in a scrap
Then that was fine too cos
If I was willing to be black
He was ready to be blue

Back in the day
Roller skates were the craze
Forget them eastend brothers

Rollerblades ruled the others
Scrap books and beano mags
Ice cream vans selling kids fags
Subbuteo and panini stickers
Cocktail bars and fancy liqueurs
We was poor but life was rich
You could see a lot from down the ditch

THE CHILD

The child looks up and smiles
All the clothes are in piles
Once scattered and thrown
They now lie as if once owned

He carefully picks his way through
Following an unseen path ahead to
Past the children in sinking sand
To the old circled with steel band

Without casual glance or raised brow
Unnoticed he passes somehow
He looks at their painted faces
And sees features smudged in places

The forest looms deep and vast
Trees reach out to gather his past
Broken twigs lie in green moss
Underfoot traversed instantly lost

LUKE RAWNSLEY

FLAKE

I'm lying by a pool
Sun is beating down on me
I hear a bird bright and distant
A bee weaves past my head
The breeze is exhausted
Limping past my arm hair
I'm looking at the sun now
To me it seems different
A fleck appears twisting down
It flattens and flips downward
It lands on my chest crazily
A single beautiful flake

FILTHY FIVERS

A mottled wad of filthy fivers
Shoved down our throats
Before anyone realises
That it's the rest of us
Holding the bowl
Before the vomit rises
And the con goes on and on
Like that bloody advert
You know the one
The one they did for Ariston
Uncle Pete sent down in 94
If you asked, he wasn't sure
But someone once said
It involved an ATM machine
And a stolen four by four
Dad sits idle for his giro
While mum scribbles out
Something else she can't afford
With her chewed at biro
They don't talk much anymore

What's the point?
When everyones point is sore
A heap of bills lie on the window
None to be paid
Unless we win the lottery though
The leccy was turned off
About a fortnight ago
But that's ok cos the tv
Was taken by the bailiffs
As if they'd already known
They had given up the fight
Without a punch being thrown
Sometimes I look at them
And it makes me sick
To think I could end up the same
Living hand to mouth
On the scrounge and the tick
We sit on a dirty couch
That dad nicked from the skip
He turfed off tramp and dog
That we're using it for a kip
I sometimes look at the stains

And it truly makes me wonder
If a family sat on it like us
If actually the closest they got
Was looking through
The steamed glass windows
Of a number ten bus

SHADES OF MAYBE

ROACH

Never had much money
Never had much time
The only roach
I ever smoked
Was the one that wasn't mine
Smell of burnt toast
Scratches on the tv
Wipe off coffee stains
Off a 6 month old CV
Back to the dole office
To face the same old questions
Give them fake answers
To same old suggestions
Apply for jobs
That don't even exist
Offy for cheapest cider
Then offy on the piss
If the weather is dece'
Spend it down the park
Till the sun drops low

Give the C a blast
Fall asleep on the grass
Wake up wit' wet arse
My life's a hangover
Don't stifle that handover
Scratch the surface
You'll see we're worth it
Scratch a bit deeper
You see I'm a keeper
Keep it all locked inside
Surrounded by insecurities
There's nowhere to hide
Watch your feet drown
As ya turn back the tide
We're part of same excuse
The one you give yourself
When there's nothing else to lose
Stare failure right in the face
Try get back to winning ways
Making your own plays
Break the self hate gaze
Break down the hedges

Don't be a slave to the maze
You spent time being so lost
Tripping train lines in the frost
Looking for peace and calm
Away from blades of self-harm
Just anyone to be nice to you
To see the shit you went thru
To see you're not a bad person
That you heal and not worsen
To make you truly believe
You can wear it on your sleeve
Broken down eyes to the floor
Still look up to be really sure
That behind every closed door
Is a chest of treasure and more
And one day you will find yourself
From sick boy to picture of health
All those scars now faded away
A bad memory faded to grey
Rise up from your ashes
Rise to meet a better you
The one who always walks past

The ones lying with a wet arse
Who walks past the cheap cider
Swigged down by the outsider
But who will always lend an ear
To those still hooked with fear
Cos you have walked their life
You'll pull away their knife
And turn blade to better stuff
Carve a future not so rough
Don't be burnt by the flame
Take its heat and find a name
Of a friend or a family member
A rope to save you tho slender
Love can save the good heart
Make whole again broken part
Don't forget a smile or hug
Rolling away from airborne slug
Drop the attitude and other shoe
Don't be the barrel pointing at you

LUKE RAWNSLEY

UMBRA

How dark the night
How splendid in sheath and crease
How delicious in fold and turn
How full with umbra and correction

THE FIST

My knuckles press into the dust
Head bowed shoulders hunched
Every muscled taut and strained
I drag each and every new breath
Kicking and screaming to my lungs
My heart hammers in my chest
As it pumps my anger heated blood
I look up to see him looking down
His gaze is cold and calculating
Weighing me up with hurtful intent
I feel almost sorry for his plight
As he lifts his arms to the crowd
He soaks up the applause and love
Every pore in his skin opens to it
I know that the moment is slipping
My senses are alive to this second
Movement blurs as purpose grips
My hands are weapons that destroy
He stumbles back flailing in vain
Fist crashes through breaking bone

His body contorts and twists away
I follow with a cartwheel of blows
There is nowhere to hide from this
I am forged anew by my own fury
It burns through every fibrous sinew
The flames burn away the doubt
They devour the hesitation inside
My fists made from the mountains
They strike with eternal virtue of will
From the snarling jaws of defeat
I snatch and wrestle my victory
Blood and pain are tickets punched
They are a prized memory for body

THE KEEL

Up steep up steep
Past the gambling abandon
Of the watchers keep
A blur of the spinning wheel
Twist of the nobbled fork
Stutters the rolling keel

SHADES OF MAYBE

THE ABYSS

I'm just a teenager
A younger kinda known stranger
No style to speak of but what?
Have I ever asked what you got?
I'm a brief shadow passing by
The question mark you always try
To form inside your heart and head
Just a dent at the end of the bed
Asking what am I meant to be?
Can't look past myself to see
If there's any point to any of this
As I take a dive into my own abyss

DANCING AND SITTING

A shadow gathers at the corner
Light reminds it of its own truth
They exist as inseparable entities
That highlight their own beauty
By dancing and sitting in our days
The hustle of movement or moment
They gather close to the story told
Or offer the parchment of the old
From photo memory to fresh dawn
They entwine our conscious heart
With feelings of love and also pain
The resonance of everything we are
Is always deep in shadows and light

THE SUN ON MY BACK

The sun is on my back
Persuading direction with each ray
My now weary feet clamber upward
Into the fiery bracken with burning memories
Of my sore and bloody feet
Into the old apple grove
That housed my mind and young blood
My old shadow flits under elms and bough
Sometimes setting off like quick silver
Diving deep into the long grass
There beneath a twisted finger
Whose leafy palms smudge a part of heaven

Tossed to the gambling winds
Thoughts seek a perspective roost
Though wings are withered and skeletal things
They alight from tender feelings
Could memory fan its own mortal wick
Where innocence once danced for all
Saving only a smile to mark its game

That look held still despite a life spent
As this day would bend and rise anew
To weary and yet so familiar ways
Nothing really ever changes it's true
Idle moments frittered by youth so fickle

Once I was taught and now I teach
In truth it becomes harder to say
For silken touch time traded a leathered hide
Now my hearts drum beats without conviction
Forward time marches without me in step
Each breath is tasted by my lungs
Though everything is dulled by a million tastes
My mind still feasts on forgotten foods
Because the child never truly dies
For it will forever carry a fiendish hunger
But now so old I can only sigh
As I reluctantly turn the last page

LUKE RAWNSLEY

BLACK AND BLACK

In the beginning there was no colour
Not a single colour to be found
So God decided to make a rainbow
And bent it bow-like to the earth

He gave every creature he made
Their own hue that wouldn't go dull
He painted the country so vast
A myriad of shades to last forever

Then when all the colours were spent
The devil pulled one out from a sleeve
It had no warmth or shine to give
Had always been where monsters are

God took it and cast it far away
Maybe to consider in a distant time
So, it slipped slowly to mother earth
And there it began its strange life

Black, black and still more black

It filled the largest and smallest crevice
It burrowed through mountains right to the core
It consumed the pebbles on the beach

And even more black, and black and black
It painted night skies and the coal pile
It had many children and called them grey
Who rode clouds while they frolicked

And even the stars wanted their company
And mass array to be between
God did indeed look upon again
So pleased he set it to every world

Now the universe is filled with black
But let us not forget from where
For though shouldered with brothers still
It seems that it will always hide

FAREWELL MOTHER, FAREWELL

My hand is empty beyond belief
My heart aching without relief
Tears have passed to a saltless flow
Leaving the emotions unsure where to go

Clouds drifting past do not acknowledge me
As I ask why to them desperately
And the blue in the sky is but a façade
The stones under my feet, suddenly too hard

Mum, mummy these words are painful when said
Because now they will only fall on ears of the dead
My mum, my mum, why did you leave me alone?
Why must I reap this bitter cruel harvest you've sown?

I have brothers and sisters to share the pain
Whose own meaning is shelter
from this strange rain
We're all looking to understand
this ghostly reflection

As it surrenders its familiarity to
an unknown complexion

A resting place lies to fit like a glove
For a body that once hugged and whispered love
How could I ever of felt comfort from this cold form
Think that its embrace could wrestle
me from the storm

But I'm crying and mumbling now like an innocent
To my dear mother, mourning the moments
that are now spent
I can say her name out loud, but it sounds so weird
Now that a motherless life through
the mist has appeared

She is again holding my hand and
I'm laughing in the sun
As our spirits find the freedom that has for us begun
Together at last we leave our shadows on Cokesford
Taking our weight of mortal earth
as we float heavenward

SHADES OF MAYBE

A poem in memory of my mother x

LUKE RAWNSLEY

SHADES OF MAYBE

LUKE RAWNSLEY

SHADES OF MAYBE

LUKE RAWNSLEY

SHADES OF MAYBE

LUKE RAWNSLEY

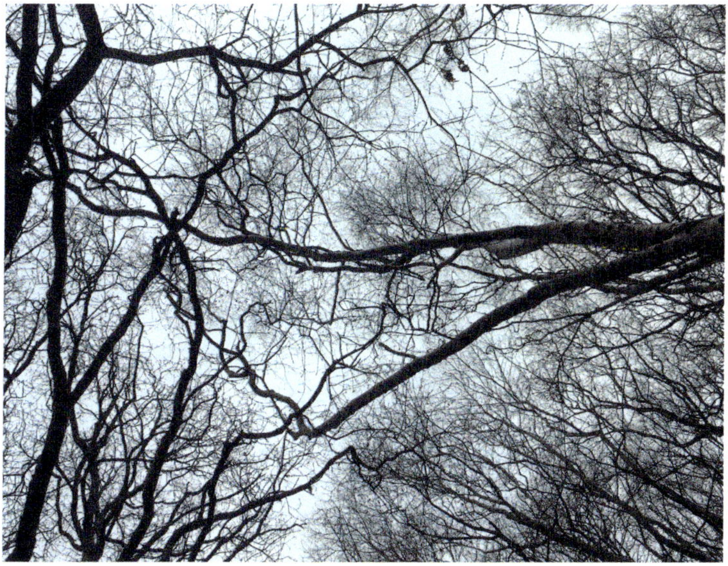

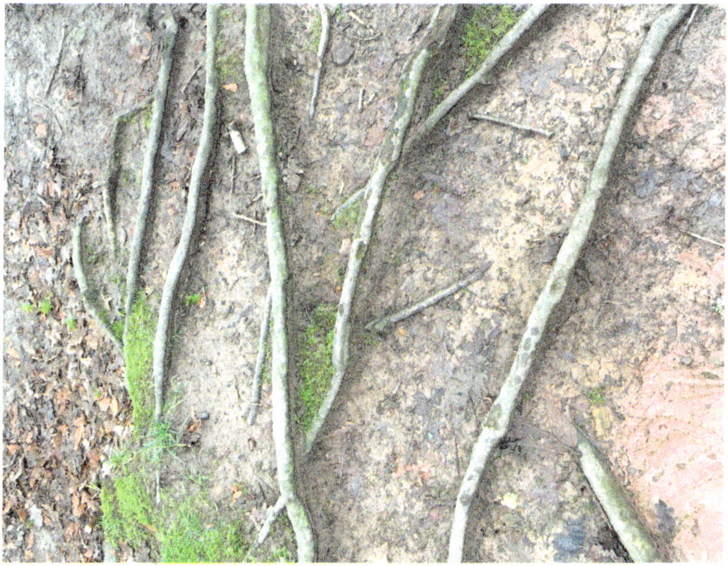

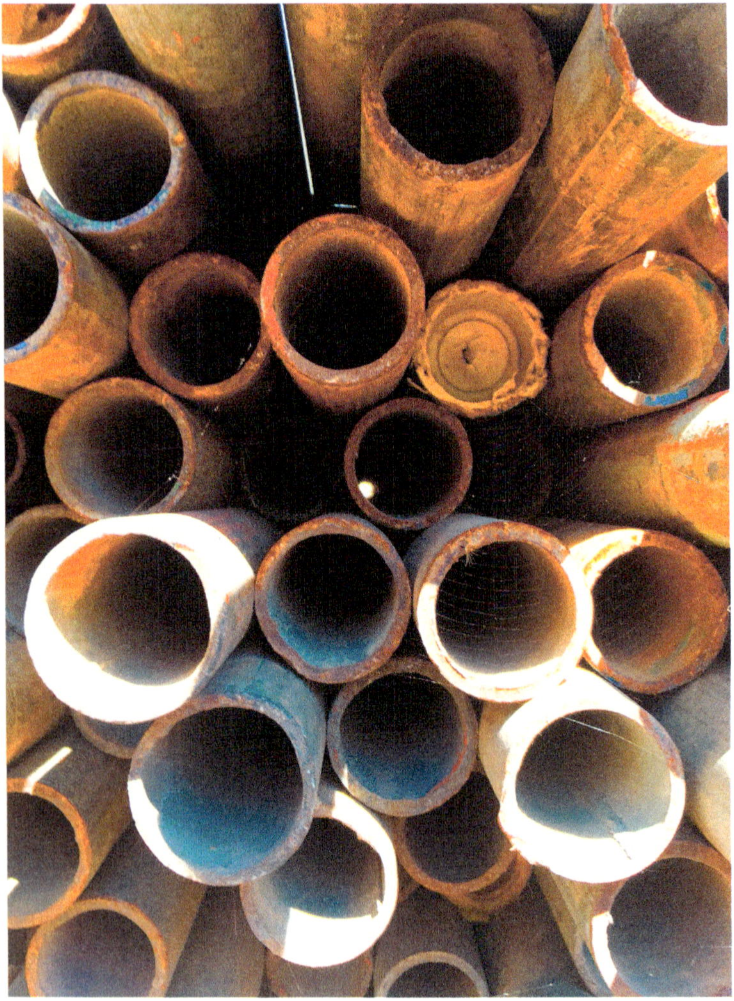

SHADES OF MAYBE

LUKE RAWNSLEY

SHADES OF MAYBE

LUKE RAWNSLEY

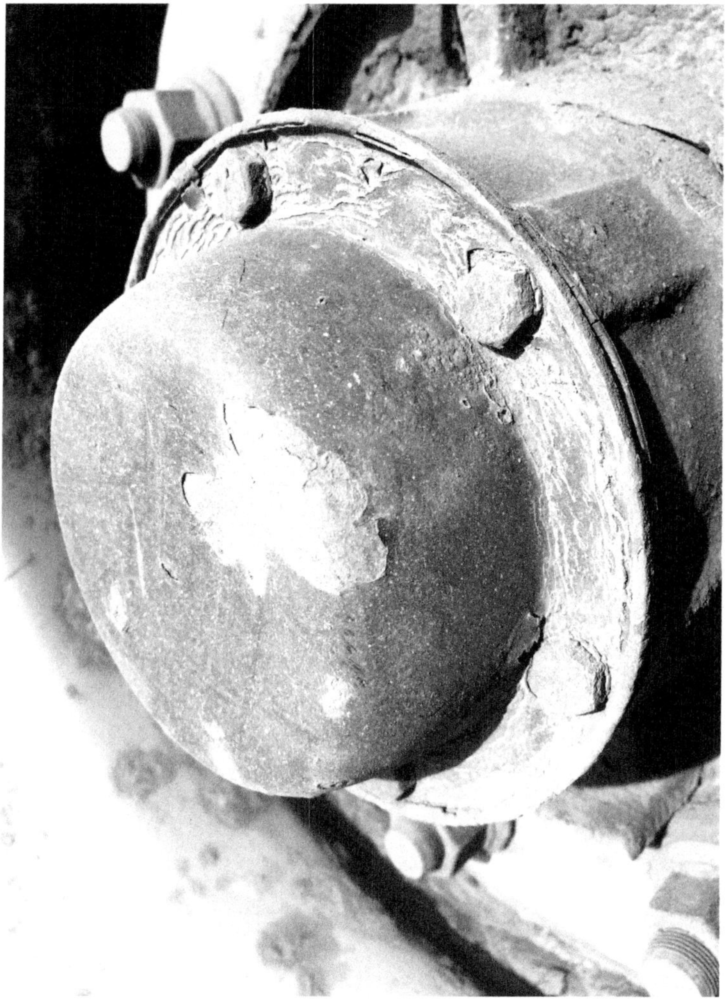

LUKE RAWNSLEY

SHADES OF MAYBE

ABOUT THE AUTHOR

Luke Rawnsley

Born 1971, in Market Deeping Lincolnshire, Luke Rawnsley is the youngest of six children. He lived with his mother and five siblings in rural Norfolk in a small village where some of his happiest memories were made. Both parents were a creative influence on him from an early age and are still a source of inspiration for him that lasts to this day. Now with two children of his own, he currently lives in Merseyside where he continues to write poetry and paint.

Printed in Great Britain
by Amazon